W9-BIR-663

The Gift of Time
Making the Most of Your Time and Your Life

by T. Alexander Anderson

Category: Time-Psychological Aspects/Conduct of Life
Time Management/Quality of Life
ISBN: 0-9706856-0-2
LCCN: 00-111548
CIP: BF637.T5A53 2001
Dewey Decimal: 158.1A

Pub Date: August 2000
Price: $15.95
Pages: 128
Trim Size: 6 1/2 x 6 1/2
Binding: Hardcover Sewn
Illustrated: 51 Photographs
Photographer: Bob Firth

First Printing: 10,000 copies
Advertising Budget: $10,000.00
Publisher: TMPress, 7455 France Ave. S. #195
Edina, MN 55435
Rights: TMPress, 952-848-2188
Agent: James Knapp
Distributer: Landauer Corporation
800-557-2144

The Gift of Time

The Gift of Time

Making the Most of Your Time and Your Life

by
T. Alexander Anderson

TMPress, Inc.

Published by TMPress, Inc.
7455 France Avenue South, #195, Edina, MN 55435

TMPress Web site: http://www.booksontime.com

Distributed to the trade by Landauer Corporation
Cumming, Iowa 50061
800/557-2144
Printed in China
First Edition
Designed by Mark Shafer

TMPress books may be purchased for educational, business, or sales promotional use.
For information write: TMPress, Inc.
Marketing Department, 7455 France Avenue South, #195, Edina, MN 55435

Library of Congress Cataloging-in-Publication data
Anderson, T. Alexander
The Gift of Time: making the most of your time and your life
T. Alexander Anderson, 1st ed.
p. cm
LCCN: 00-111548
ISBN: 0-9706856-0-2
!. Time--Psychological aspects. 2. Time management.
3. Conduct of life. 4. Quality of life. I. Title.
158. 1A   BF637.T5A53 2001
10 9 8 7 6 5 4 3 2 1

The Gift of Time is dedicated
to my son, Shawn,
who has given me my life's
most precious moments.

ACKNOWLEDGEMENTS
I would like to thank the following people
who assisted me in the creation of this book:
Jim Knapp, my agent, for his wisdom and guidance;
Landauer corporation for distributing to the trade;
Margie Adler for her editorial skills, enthusiasm, insight and support;
Mark Shafer for his talented and creative design work.
Nancy Firth for her valuable assistance;
Herb Fredrick for his thoughtful input, editing, and honest friendship;
and Tom Kinn for his professional perceptions and belief in this project.

A special thanks to Bob Firth for his incredible photography and
artistic input. Bob Firth has been an award winning photographer for over thirty years.
A leading Minnesota stock and assignment photographer he is best known for
his large format images of nature, landscapes and scenics.
His work has graced ths covers of more than four hundred periodicals and appeared in
National Geographic, National Wildlife, The New Yorker, and *Outside Magazine.*
In addition he has done a variety of books, calendars, and postcards.
He lives in Chaska, Minnesota with his wife Nancy and their two sons.

Photo Credits
All photographs by Bob Firth except on
pages 18, 53, and 59 by T. Alexander Anderson; photo on page 55 by Bob Clauss;
inside back cover photo by Catherine Wickham.

Once upon a time

there was no time...

Contents

ON A DISTANT BEACH NOT SO LONG AGO,
a quiet breeze dusted my face with the salt air as I sat at the water's
ever-changing edge. While the waves gently brushed the soles of my
bare feet, my mind, body, and heart came into sync with the rhythm of
the sea. In that moment, I felt totally alive and connected to the
soul of the world. The realization that many timeless moments had
presented themselves but escaped me turned the joy behind my tears
into sadness and I grieved the loss.

I had been living a life starved for time. My schedule had been full, but
my time felt empty. By focusing my attention on the clock, I had missed
what was precious in the moment. With each glance at the clock, I
perceived a hidden message: time was running out. Fear of not having
enough time drove me. I had allowed the clock to control my life.

In that one moment on the beach, I became aware of the gift of the present moment and transformed my relationship with time. As I moved my consciousness to the moment and away from the clock my experience of life changed. I began to feel more alive.

In the succeeding years, I would uncover many more remarkable gifts that would reinforce my new relationship with time and help me create a more fulfilling life. *The Gift of Time* contains these gifts. They are accompanied by questions and ideas that guided me to a greater understanding of time and helped give my life deeper meaning.

As you come to understand these insights, it is my hope that you, too, will discover the gift of time is the present moment—and is richer than you ever dreamed.

GIFTS OF THE PAST
Remembering and Letting Go

"The past is but the
beginning of a beginning,
and all that is and has been
is but the twilight of the dawn."

—*H. G. Wells*

Call to mind your earliest memory.

Memories are the dreams we all carry with us.

We can evoke memories by visiting a special place from our past.

Make a visit to a childhood home, a park

where you once played, or a school you formerly attended.

Take time for reflection and contemplation of

early memories that still impact your life today.

"There is no time like the old times,

when you and I were young."

— *Oliver Wendell Holmes*

THE GIFT OF TIME

We were given memories

so we could smile in our twilight years.

Picture yourself

years from now,

quietly sitting

on a bench

under a tree

overlooking a park.

The sun is setting

in the silence

of the evening hour.

You smile as you

reflect on your life.

What is your smile about?

Today's crisis can be the seed of tomorrow's laughter.

What is your funniest memory?

Keeping a journal is a way to capture precious memories
we may otherwise forget.

Keep a journal.

Write in it for 21 days,

even if you write just one sentence a day.

Read it at a later time, and note the thoughts

you would have forgotten had you not written them down.

Consider making writing a ritual.

If your past seems to change,

it may be because your beliefs evolve

or your memory evaporates.

Momentos help us verify our past.

What are the most treasured possessions of your past?

Imagine you are looking across an open field.

You see a child a hundred yards away walking toward you,—

As the child nears, you realize that child is you—

the little person you once were. You gaze into each other's eyes

and connect with the child's innocent, imaginative soul.

You wonder if you are what that child wanted to become.

Is there some sadness you feel about your life?

What is it about?

What are your deepest regrets?

Can you do anything about them now?

When we look back on our life,

we regret the things we did not do

more than the things we did and

wish we had taken more risks.

Sand cannot flow up the hourglass.

"*If Only*" keeps us trapped in the past.
"*What If*" keeps us trapped in the future.

Replace "*If Only*" with "*Even Though.*"
Replace "*What If*" with "*Even If.*"

When we dwell on the past using words like
shoulda, woulda, and *coulda,* we
let yesterday take up today.
The past becomes a prison because
we choose to live in it.
The less we look back on life,
the more we will move forward.

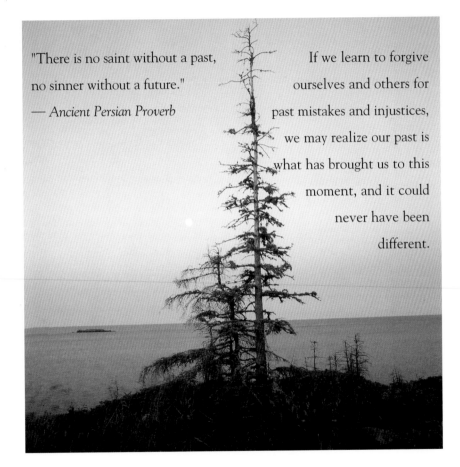

"There is no saint without a past, no sinner without a future."
— *Ancient Persian Proverb*

If we learn to forgive ourselves and others for past mistakes and injustices, we may realize our past is what has brought us to this moment, and it could never have been different.

"Let the past drift away with the water."

— *Japanese Saying*

Envision all your mistakes inside a helium-filled balloon.

You are holding onto the string as tightly as you can.

Slowly, release your grip,

and watch the balloon float away

until it is out of sight.

. . . .

"No matter how difficult the past

you can always begin again today."

— *Buddha*

You cannot change the past,

but you can change how it affects the future.

GIFTS FOR SLOWING DOWN

Finding Serenity in a Hurried World

"The journey is the destination."

—*Unknown*

We are often in such a hurry to get to our destination,
we forget to look for the magnificence in the journey.
We hurry because we are holding onto an illusion
that life in the fast lane will get us to our destination sooner.
We think our destination is happiness, and as we rush to
find happiness we pass it by. Happiness can only
be experienced in the present moment.
The journey is filled with such moments;
the destination has few.

Most of our sense of
urgency is exaggerated.
Whenever we are feeling hurried,
we are carrying negative emotions, such as: fear,
anger, impatience, frustration, anxiety, and resentment.
As these emotions race through our mind,
they undermine our health, and the time we saved
by rushing is often spent recuperating.

"The wise man is never in a hurry."
— *Aristotle*

We are afraid,

if we slow down our life,

we will fall behind.

Life is not a race.

It is not time, but the measuring of time

that causes us so much distress.

Just for fun, check the time. Close your eyes,

and without counting, guess when two minutes are up.

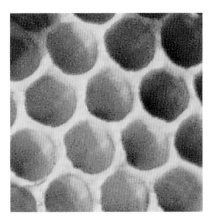

Do your days and their activities blur?

When we are rushing, our life feels insane.

At the precise moment we admit we cannot

keep up with the pace of the world,

we not only stop the insanity—we invite serenity.

"Wisely and slowly;

they stumble that run fast."

—*William Shakespeare*

Slow down.

You will be surprised to find

how often you can get there sooner.

GIFTS FOR SLOWING DOWN

When we hurry, our breathing is short and shallow.
To slow the speed of our life we must first slow our breath.
It is the one vital body function we can control.
We can use our breath to slow our pace any time we choose.

Follow your breath as you inhale deeply
into your abdomen; fill it up.
Continue with the same breath to fill
your diaphragm, and lastly, your lungs.
Your whole inhalation should last about six seconds.
Without pausing, follow your breath
as you exhale completely for the count of six.
Continue this for one minute and notice if you feel
a greater sense of calm and awareness.

The Gift of Time

The faster we live,

and the more we try to squeeze into our time,

the less time we feel we have.

We set the time traps that ensnare us

by trying to pack in too many events and errands

in too short a time-frame.

Write the word "s-l-o-w-l-y" on three sticky notes.

Place one on your bathroom mirror,

another one on your car dashboard,

and the last one in your work environment.

Use these notes as an anchor to remind you, if you are racing, to take

some deep breaths and relax.

"It doesn't matter how slowly you go
as long as you do not stop."

—*Confucius*

Act as if you have plenty of time,
and you will begin to feel
like you have plenty of time.
For the rest of the day,
walk at a slower pace than normal.
Pay attention to how you feel
at the end of the day.

When we give ourselves extra time,

we slow down the speed of our life.

Next week every time you drive,

no matter where your destination,

leave ten minutes earlier than usual.

Place a calming fragrance in your car;

listen to relaxing music,

and do not exceed the speed limit.

"Rest is not idleness, and to lie sometimes
on the grass under the trees on a summer's day,
listening to the murmur of the water,
or watching the clouds float across the sky,
is by no means a waste of time."
—*Sir J. Lubbock*

A rested mind is open to acts of love, kindness,
compassion, tenderness, patience, and understanding.

THE GIFT OF TIME

We act as if time is our master, but it is our mystery.

Imagine time suddenly stands still for the whole world.

The clocks are stopped,

and the whole world is freeze-framed

except for you.

How much time would you want to lapse

before the world starts again?

What would you do during this time?

A good book, like a good meal,

is meant to be savored.

Are you speed-reading this book?

What is the rush?

Allow yourself to read *The Gift of Time* slowly.

Take a few slow, deep breaths.

Give yourself time for contemplation.

GIFTS FOR AWARENESS

Paying Attention and Creating Clarity

"Both in thought and feeling,
even though time be real,
to realize the unimportance of time
is the gate of wisdom."
—*Bertrand Russell*

Have you ever stood at the edge of an ocean, inside a forest,
or on top of a mountain, and realized how minute you are
in relation to the magnitude of the world, and at the same time,
felt connected to its power and magnificence?
It is this connection that belies the fact
that you are more powerful and magnificent
than you ever could imagine. It is then you come
to understand, if for only a brief moment,
the insignificance of time.

Do you often feel so busy that you
are unable to enjoy the now?

Attention is the intention to live in the present.
It is not what we do that matters;
it is how we pay attention to what we are doing.
Awareness is what makes moments unforgettable.
When we experience life to the fullest,
it is because we are paying attention.

Many of us do not focus and attend
to our experiences because we are afraid that
if we do, we might miss something
somewhere else.

We need to forget about where we are not
and pay attention to the miracles of where we are.
If we do not pay attention to the here and now,
we could miss everything.

Wisdom comes from paying attention.

Everyone you talk with deserves your complete attention.
Listen not only with your ears, but with your eyes, mind, and heart.
Concentrate on that person's whole being and you will see
not only the essence of their soul, but yours as well.

What we pay attention to are often clues to how
we really want to spend our time.
These clues can lead us to our life's purpose.

For the next week make a list
of what attracts your attention,
no matter how seemingly insignificant it appears.

With an increasing number of stimuli competing for our attention, it is getting more difficult to find the joy of being in the present moment. We need to eliminate as many distractions as we can, and ignore the rest.

Plan a dining event just for yourself. Turn off your stereo, television, phone, and other communication devices. Let go of all your concerns.
Make this meal your only focus.
Create a beautiful place setting on your dining table and use your best dishes. Prepare your favorite meal with all the trimmings.
When you are ready to eat, take a moment to pause in gratitude.
Notice the colors and shapes of your food.
Deeply inhale the aromas. As you eat, relish not only the taste, but the temperature and texture. Eat slowly, and savor each bite.
When you are finished, sit a few minutes, and allow your food to settle.

"When you walk just walk—when you eat just eat." —*Buddha*

A man with a watch knows what time it is.

A man with two watches can never be sure.

— Segal's Law

The time you spend counting time

is time that does not count.

If you have an hourly alarm on your watch, set it.

Let it be a bell to bring you into the moment.

"Take time to work; it's the price of success.

Take time to think; it's the source of power.

Take time to play; it's the secret of perpetual youth.

Take time to read; it's the foundation of wisdom.

Take time to be friendly; it's the road to happiness.

Take time to dream; it's hitching your wagon to a star.

Take time to love and be loved; it's the privilege of the gods.

Take time to look around; it's too short a day to be selfish.

Take time to laugh; it's the music of the soul."

—*Old English prayer*

We do not need to learn how to live.

We need to remember.

GIFTS OF RHYTHMS AND CYCLES

Finding Continuity in Chaos

"To every thing there is a season,
and time to every purpose under the heaven:
A time to be born, and a time to die;
a time to plant,
and a time to pluck up that which is planted;
A time to kill, and a time to heal;
a time to break down, and a time to build up;
A time to weep, and a time to laugh;
a time to mourn, and a time to dance:
A time to cast away stones,
and time to gather stones together;
a time to embrace, and a time to refrain
from embracing:
A time to get, and a time to lose;
a time to keep, and a time to cast away;
A time to rend, and a time to sew;
a time to keep silence, and a time to speak;
A time to love, and a time to hate;
a time of war, and a time of peace."

—*The Bible, Ecclesiastes 3: 1-8*

Nothing stays the same; nothing.

"There is no season such delight can bring

As summer, autumn, winter, and the spring."

—*William Browne*

What do you look forward to each season?

Rituals are like seasons.

They bring continuity into our lives.

Rituals can include prayers,

bedtime stories, family gatherings,

movie nights, Sunday brunches,

and weekly tennis matches.

What rituals do you have in your life?

What rituals have you forfeited

that you would like to renew?

Rituals are like habits.

Are there rituals in your life you need to break

or change?

"Adopt the pace of nature,
her secret is patience."
—*Ralph Waldo Emerson*

What ways are you synchronized with nature?
Maybe you feel crazy when there is a full moon,
anxious during a storm, or lazy on a hot summer day.

Time is both linear and cyclical;

it is full of rhythms,

repetition and recurrence.

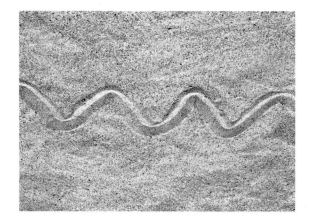

Our heart is the timepiece of our body.

We need to listen to it.

Put two pendulum clocks next to each other,

and eventually they will synchronize.

Are you in sync with your partner or

other people with whom you spend a lot of time?

If not, does this cause problems in your relationships?

THE GIFT OF TIME
....

Many of us deprive ourselves of sleep

so we can cram one more activity into our day.

The repercussions are that we

miss many of the gifts each day brings

because we are too tired to notice them.

When we are tired, it is difficult to be aware.

We need to get plenty of sleep;

we need to honor our body's rhythms and cycles.

"With every ending there is a new beginning."

—*Unknown*

When we embrace endings and welcome beginnings,

we are less likely to get stuck in transitions.

GIFTS OF AGE
AND ACCEPTANCE

Knowing There Is Enough Time

"I still find each day too short for all the thoughts I want to think,
all the walks I want to take, all the books I want to read,
and all the friends I want to see."
—*John Burroughs*

Most of us believe there is not enough time. This belief causes us to hurry.
The more we hurry, the less time we feel we have.
The less time we feel we have, the more often we affirm our belief
that we do not have enough time.
We do not have enough time to do everything we want,
but we have enough time to do anything we want.
Next time you are affirming you do not have enough time,
use the following affirmation instead:
"I have all the time I need to do whatever I choose."
It will remind you to focus on your priorities
and keep you from becoming a victim of the clock.

Which thought is most disturbing to you?
You believe you have either too much time or not enough.

Most of us use one of two excuses for not living our life:
One, "There is plenty of time."
The other, "It is too late."
What is your excuse?

"To live is so startling

it leaves little time for anything else."

— *Emily Dickinson*

Some people live their lives with such passion that

they never wish for a different life or a longer one.

Those who live life to the fullest

are least afraid to die, because they know

they have not wasted their time.

Our bodies grow old and die, but our spirit is timeless.
It soars in the lives we touch.

What would you like to leave behind when
you depart from this world that would resist becoming
buried in the sands of time?

We never know which day will be our last.

Imagine you will die in five minutes.
There is nothing you can do to save yourself.
You have a pen and paper to write your final thoughts.
To whom would you write, and what would you say?
Try writing these thoughts now.

"Every man desires to live long;

but no man would be old.'

— *Jonathan Swift*

Many of us complain of growing old

while so many never get the chance.

There are worse things than growing old.

As we age, we must remember that if we spend

too much time mourning the loss of our youth

or trying to keep it, we will miss living

what could be the best part of our life.

We age gracefully by enjoying each moment,

appreciating the time we are given,

and giving our time to others.

— *57* —

"When your friends begin to flatter

you on how young you look,

it is a sure sign you are getting older."

—*Mark Twain*

Fifty is a lot younger than it used to be,

and many of us feel too young to get old.

How old do you think you look?

How old do you feel psychologically?

"In youth we learn, in age we understand."

—*Marie Von Ebner-Eschenbach*

Age does not wrinkle our soul.

It enriches it.

As sand flows through the hourglass of life,

we can see through it more clearly.

GIFTS FOR PATIENCE

Learning Patience

"The reward of patience is patience."

—*St. Augustine*

Each day
brings us lessons
that will teach us patience.
Next time you feel impatient,
take note of any physical
symptoms in your body.
Maybe you will feel
your abdomen tighten, heart race,
neck stiffen, or head ache.
Let these symptoms
remind you to take a deep breath
and ask for patience.

"With time and patience
the mulberry leaf
becomes a silk gown."
—*Chinese Proverb*

True artists do not hurry when they are creating,
for they know rushing will diminish not only their work,
but also their love of the work.
A great work of art can take a long time.
What silk gowns have you created in your life?
What would you like to create?

THE GIFT OF TIME

We cannot stand having a patient driver
in front of us and appreciate him
when he is behind us.

Impatience is a form of anger about the theft of our time.
Remember: For every minute we remain impatient,
we give up 60 seconds worth of peace of mind.

Next time someone cuts
in front of you on the freeway,
instead of becoming angry or upset,
consider there is a medical emergency
and they need to get to the hospital.
You are helping them get there faster
by allowing them space in front of you.
Who knows? You may be right.

Patience is one of the most difficult things

for a child to learn from a parent,

and one of the most important things

a parent can learn from a child.

"Have patience with all things,

but chiefly have patience with yourself."

—*Saint Francis de Sales*

"The secret of patience is to do
something else in the meantime."

—*Anonymous*

There will always be delays in life.
Accept this, and waiting becomes much easier.
See waiting as an unexpected gift of time for yourself.
List three things you can do to enjoy time spent waiting.

"Strength comes from waiting."

—José Manti

Next time someone behind you

in line at the store has few items to your many,

step back and let them have your place in line.

Notice how you feel.

THE GIFT OF TIME

"Anything worth having is worth waiting for."

—*Old proverb*

"If it is worth waiting for, it is worth having now.'

—*Newer Proverb*

Instant gratification is rarely as satisfying

as delayed gratification.

"Most overnight successes

take 10 to 20 years."

—*Anonymous*

When our lives are not coming together

as quickly as we would like,

there is a reason.

Sometimes the reason is simply

a lesson in patience.

GIFTS FOR BALANCE
AND SIMPLICITY

Becoming Centered and Contented

It is challenging to create a balanced life
because the speed of life is accelerating
in a world with an increasing number of distractions.

When there is a lot
of movement and change in our life,
we need to look at the stillness of the world.
Try resting near a large rock next time you feel overwhelmed. Press
your hands on it and notice its steadfastness and dependability.
Allow its weight and power to ground you
to the core of the earth.

Most of us fill up our schedules
with work, errands, and obligations.
If there is any time remaining,
we spend it on ourselves.
If we are looking for balance
in our lives, we need to
schedule time for ourselves first.
It can be time for exercise,
meditation, contemplation,
learning, playing,
or doing anything
we love.

THE GIFT OF TIME

For people who are afraid of free time,
it is difficult to endure an empty hour.
We can feel anxious, restless, or lonely.
These feelings are uncomfortable; but, if we live
with this discomfort long enough, it will pass.

Free time is nothing to be ashamed of.
To sit still for even a few minutes and experience
the simplicity of feeling alive is not a waste of time.
Give yourself permission this week to be
with nature for a couple of hours.
Listen for the songs of the birds.
Feel the coolness of the breeze.
Smell the freshness of the air.
Taste a wild berry,
or gaze at the beauty
of the wild flowers.

Leisure time may
require practice and discipline, especially,
if we have not enjoyed any for awhile.

When our bodies are no longer rushing, our minds
can still be racing and our leisure time will feel stressful.
When our leisure time feels stressful,
it is no longer leisure time.

Next time you notice your mind racing, know the stressful thoughts
that creep into your mind will drift out.

THE GIFT OF TIME

We all know people who stay busy to feel worthy.

Busyness is not a status symbol.

If we stay busy all the time, we become "human doings"

instead of "human beings."

In the next 24 hours, create time to light a candle,

put on soft music and prepare a warm bath.

Watch the flame flicker

as you bathe in solitude and do nothing.

Even though we are more productive
than ever before, we feel we have less time
because we are trading our time
for more goods and services.

Next time you feel like going to a shopping mall
for recreation, consider going to a nature park instead.

The Gift of Time

While communication devices and computer technology

can save time, they can also create chaos in our lives.

They increase the opportunity for interruptions

that can spoil our leisure time and

consume it as we spend time trying to figure out

how to use these devices and technologies.

Bear in mind it takes time to save time,

and the money we spend

to save time takes time to earn.

"Time is the most valuable thing

a man can spend."

—*Theophrastus*

Debt commits our time to earn money to pay for our financial past.

We need to be careful not to become slaves to the lifestyle we create.

The more we simplify our material life

the more time we will have to live.

Time isn't money.

Time is priceless.

GIFTS OF FREEWILL
Creating Time

Time is the greatest gift we are given.
The second greatest gift is the freedom
to use it anyway we choose.

We cannot change time, but we can change how we use it.
When we choose to do things we do not enjoy, like paying bills,
it is because we do not want to face the consequences of not doing them.
It is during these times we need to remember we also choose our
moods and attitudes. A good mood and a positive attitude
can make our time more pleasurable no matter what we choose to do.
Next time you sit down to pay the bills,
play some relaxing music and sip a cup of tea.

What is your least favorite way to spend time?
What is your favorite way to spend time?
Are you doing what you love most of the time?
If not, why?

If we have a sense of misusing our time
no matter how many activities we squeeze into a day,
it may be because we have been too busy to stop
and think about what matters most in our lives.

Life is not about checking off items on lists.
As you study your "to do" list, ask yourself
what impact these tasks will have on your future.
If the answer is little or none, cross it off.
Not everyone needs a "to do" list.

Some of us need "don't do" lists.
Make a list of things you no longer want to do and
you will discover more time to do what you like.

The Gift of Time

The happiness of our lives may well depend
on the quality of our time.

Quality time is nurturing your body and soul.
Quality time is freeing your mind of negative thought
so you can receive the gifts of the moment.
Quality time is dreaming, even if you are awake.
Quality time is feeling intimate connections with others.
Quality time is experiencing the wonders of nature.
Quality time is searching for your life's purpose
and living it once you find it.

"He is only rich who owns the day.
The days are ever divine...
They are of the least pretension,
and of the greatest capacity
of anything that exists."
—*Ralph Waldo Emerson*

We are wealthy
when we spend
our days doing
what we love.

Always is never true.

Never is always false.

Eliminate "always" and "never" from your vocabulary.

These are choices in time you cannot promise.

GIFTS OF FREEWILL

"I find the best way to spending my days—
at least did long ago—is the freeway;
not to make plans, but go this path or that
as the mood dictates."

—*Walt Whitman*

Do you find the spontaneous moments
are those when you feel most alive?
Be careful not to set such a rigid schedule for
yourself that you have no room
for spontaneity.

Most of us have obligations in our life we dread.

We do not have to accept every invitation.

One of the greatest time-saving devices

is a simple, "No, thank you."

For many of us it is hard to say no.

When we do say no,

we often feel we need to offer an excuse.

Saying "No thank you" is enough.

It is not necessary to make up excuses.

"Time management is of little value
for people who are not spending their time
according to their values."

—*Unknown*

Make an appointment with yourself one week from today
to put your values in writing. Use this week to think about
what your values are.

GIFTS FOR THE FUTURE

Turning Dreams into Reality

"The best thing about the future
is that it comes one day at a time."
—*Abraham Lincoln*

Describe your perfect day
from the minute you awaken
until the minute you fall asleep.
Place your perfect day in your calendar.
Do not let anything or anyone,
including yourself, keep you
from living this day.

"Our children are our future."
—*Unknown*

If you created a time capsule to be opened
in fifty years by your grandchildren,
what three items of present day society would you place in it?

"If you wait for tomorrow, tomorrow comes;

If you don't wait for tomorrow, tomorrow comes."

—*Senegalese Proverb*

If you had a machine to travel ahead in time,

how many years into the future would you go?

What would you hope to discover?

Our life is meant to be spent living our dreams.

If we do not live our dreams, we will

live the dreams of others.

You may find the following

activity enlightening and fun.

Gather all your favorite magazines,

including the ones you have not had time to read.

Cut out pictures, phrases, and words

that remind you of your dreams.

With glue and poster board,

design a collage with your cut-outs.

When you finish, place it where you can see it every day.

"The possibilities for tomorrow

are usually beyond our expectations."

—*Anonymous*

Too often we put off our long-term dreams

for our short-term desires.

If you easily lose sight of your dreams,

try cutting a note card to the size of a credit card.

Write your greatest dream for your life on the card.

Keep in mind you can never dream too big.

Place it in your wallet so every time you open it

your dream is there to remind you of your life's destination.

Let it also be there to remind you to save money for your dream.

Fear of the future blocks our imagination.

Sometimes we do not seek the life we want

because we are afraid we will fail.

It is better to live our life as a failure

doing something we love than to be

a success at something we dislike.

Our future is determined

by our thoughts, beliefs, and actions.

If you are not living the life you want,

what are you afraid of?

If we want to make the most of our time,

we need to think ahead.

A written mission statement can be the map for your

path in life, and give your time greater significance.

If you do not already have one,

try writing a mission statement for your life.

Make sure it aligns with your values;

remain open to change and refinement.

As you change, so may your mission.

If you cannot articulate a mission statement,

dedicate time to discovering one.

Your goals are the
measuring sticks of your
time. When you pen your
goals for one month, one
year, and five years from now,
you crystallize them and
they become more real.
Make sure they align with
your values and mission.

It is important to prioritize
your goals. Your first
priority is to keep
your first priority
your first priority.

THE GIFT OF TIME

"There is no time like the present
to determine your future."
—*Unknown*

Too many of us spend our lives getting ready to live.
We spend our lives planning without acting.
When we do act, we become distracted
and forget our intentions.
If we take time each month to review our progress in life,
we can save a lot of time and avoid getting sidetracked.

Instead of concerning yourself with the time,
ask yourself; "Is the time I am spending
contributing to my life's intention and enhancing
my health and happiness?"

"First I was dying to finish high school and start college

And then I was dying to finish college and start working

Then I was dying to marry and have children

Then I was dying for my children to grow old enough

for school so I could return to work

Then I was dying to retire.

And now, I'm dying—and suddenly

I realize I forgot to live."

—*Unknown*

Try to write your epitaph in ten words or less.

GIFTS OF DOING

Making Life Happen

"Lives of great men all remind us,
we can make our lives sublime,
And, departing, leave behind us
Footprints on the sands of time."
—*Henry Wadsworth Longfellow*

We must get off our "buts" to place
footprints in the sands of time.

Some of us spend time making up excuses,

when we could have spent this time

avoiding the need to make them.

Are there chores in your life that cost

you more time because you are avoiding,

rather than doing them?

"You think you have time."

—*Buddha*

Given the choice, most of us choose delay over action.
We procrastinate because we believe doing nothing
will be less painful than doing what we need to do.
Consider the consequences as well as the pain
of action versus inaction.

Thinking we have plenty of time in our life
can lead to procrastination, and procrastination—
as responsibilities pile up—can lead us to think
we do not have enough time.

Besides the skill of getting things done,
there is the skill of leaving things undone.
Sometimes the tasks we put off never need doing.
Notice and eliminate the non-essentials.

Fill in the blank: Someday I will ....

Now, erase the word "Someday."

"Later comes sooner than you think."

—Proverb

Regrets are the price of procrastination.

Imagine you are looking back

at your life ten years from now.

What regrets would you hate to have?

Misuse of time may be the most noteworthy cause
for unhappiness and failure.

We all think we misuse our time.
When we do, we need to remember
what matters most and invest our time accordingly.

THE GIFT OF TIME
....

Doing nothing can be the most significant time we spend.
Our best thoughts come out of doing nothing.
For the next five minutes, put down this book
and do nothing except allow your thoughts to wander.

Spending time doing nothing can be difficult.
If you are resisting this exercise, ask yourself why.

"All things come to those who wait...

They come, but often too late."

—*Lady Mary M. Currie*

Do you let things happen

or do you make things happen?

"Sow an act and you reap a habit.
Sow a habit and you reap a character.
Sow a character and you reap a destiny."
—*Samuel Smiles*

It is our actions that
determine our destiny.

"A stitch in time saves nine."

— *English Proverb*

Do you have seams in any of your relationships

that need mending?

Think of three people you want to call,

but have not because of lack of time.

Call them this week.

THE GIFT OF TIME

A 72-year-old man told his son
he is going to begin college and get his degree.
His son thought his father was going senile and told him,
"But, Dad you will be 76 when you graduate!"
The father responded by saying,
"Son, I will be 76 in four years,
whether or not I go to college."

We will never be younger than we are today.
If we wait for the perfect opportunity to do something,
we may miss the opportunity forever.

Are there any missed opportunities that haunt you?
Write them down on a sheet of paper.
Look beyond your limiting beliefs
and ask yourself if the opportunities still exist.
Look for possibilities and take advantage of them.

The "whys" of the past and the "whens"
of the future are not as important
as the "whats" of the present.

What can you do today
that will have significance tomorrow?

GIFTS FOR BEING

*Doing Less and
Being More*

If we love time
rather than fear it,
time becomes our friend,
not our enemy.

If you perceive time as your enemy,
how would your life change if you saw it as your friend?

"If something is boring after
two minutes, try it for four.
If it is still boring, try it for eight,
sixteen, thirty-two and so on.
Eventually, one discovers that
it is not boring, but very interesting."

—*Zen saying*

What bores you that people you know enjoy?
Ask them why they enjoy it.

"The gem cannot be polished without friction,
nor man perfected without trials."
—*Confucius*

It is our most difficult times
that define who we are.

We all go through life learning different

lessons at different times.

We need to accept our current state of innocence

and the learning curve of others.

We are exactly where we need to be

in time and space right now.

We need to appreciate the moment we have

instead of shaming ourselves for either

what we think we should be doing this moment,

or should have been doing in the past.

THE GIFT OF TIME
....

Worry is a waste of time,
and most of our worries never happen.
You can save time worrying by asking yourself,
"Will what I am worrying about make any difference
ten years from now?"
If it won't, don't worry.

"Instead of worrying, try praying."
—*Unknown*

If we are busy judging others,

we do not have time to love them.

If we gossip about someone else's life,

we waste our life.

If we spend time trying to change others,

it costs us time that we could be using to change

the only person we can truly change, ourself.

If we spend our time improving ourself,

then we have no time to disapprove of others.

The only person we need compare

ourselves to is who we were yesterday.

"The deepest principle in human nature
is the craving to be appreciated."
—*William James*

Take time to find the good in others.
Take time to acknowledge and appreciate
the actions of those you love.
At least once a day show someone your love.
Give that person a hug, a gentle pat on the back, a kiss, a smile,
or a thoughtful letter. Your world will change.

Gifts for Being

"Fifty years from
now it will not matter
what kind of car you drove,
which kind of house you lived in,
how much you had in your bank account,
nor what your clothes looked like.
But the world will be a little better
because you were important
in the life of a child."

—*Anonymous*

Never miss a chance to give a child
a few minutes of your time.
The gift of time is the gift of love.
Some people go through life without ever
having been told they were loved by their parents.
We need to tell our children we love them often.

— *113* —

"If you are going to spend time alone,
make sure you enjoy the company
of the one you are with."
—*Unknown*

During times of loneliness,
we feel separate from the universe.
During times of solitude, we feel connected.
We all need time for solitude.

Consider giving yourself a weekend retreat at home
or away from home. Eliminate any foreseeable interruptions
and create a nurturing ambiance with candles and aromas.
Spend this time in silence doing what you know
will be caring for your soul. It could be inspirational reading,
meditating, writing, or going for a walk.

"The shadow on the dial,
The striking of the clock...
These are but arbitrary and outward signs,
The measure of Time, but not Time itself.
Time is the Life of the Soul."
—Henry Wadsworth Longfellow

... and our soul is timeless;
that is what makes our life eternal.

Take time to nourish your soul each day
because there is no greater tragedy than when the
soul dies before the body.

Time is the most important

gift we can give or receive.

What is your favorite way to give time?

Each day make a conscious effort to give time to someone,

even if it is just to open a door.

People who are grateful for their time

seem to have enough time.

Express gratitude for the time you have.

It is your most precious present.

THE GIFT IS THE PRESENT

Making the Most of Each Moment

"Only that day dawns to which we are awake."
—*Henry David Thoreau*

Being awake to experience the bounties of life is a choice.
When we operate our life on auto-pilot,
and it feels like we are sleepwalking through our days,
it is because we do not want to wake up.

The Gift is the Present

....

"Listen to the Exhortation of the Dawn!
Look to this Day
For it is Life, the very Life of Life
In its brief course lie all the
Verities and Realities of your Existence:
The Bliss of Growth
The Glory of Action
The Splendor of Beauty
For Yesterday is but a Dream of Happiness
And every Tomorrow a Vision of Hope
Look well therefore to this Day
Such is the Salutation of the Dawn!"

—*Sanskrit Poem*

What is the first thing you think about when you wake up
in the morning? Does this set the tone for your whole day?
How do you think your life would change if you woke up
appreciating each day and asking yourself,
"What can I do to make the most of this day?"

"Recollection and anticipation

fill up most of our moments."

—*Samuel Johnson*

Cherish the moments of your past by remembering.

Enjoy future moments by anticipating.

Spend most of your time in the greatest joy of all—

the present moment.

When we want the future

to either come quickly

or the past to leave slowly,

we forget this moment is all we have.

Do you live like you are going

to live forever?

"To see a World in a Grain of Sand
And a Heaven in a Wild Flower,
Hold Infinity in the palm of your hand
And Eternity in an hour."

—*William Blake*

Make a date with yourself some night this week
to gaze at the star-filled sky and contemplate the universe.

THE GIFT IS THE PRESENT

"The present is the past's student

and the future's teacher."

—*Anonymous*

At the end of each day,

ask yourself and answer the following question:

"What have I learned today?"

Share your answer with people you care about,

and ask them what they learned.

x

"...nothing can bring back the hour
of the splendour in the grass,
of the glory in the flower."
—*William Wordsworth*

If you do not already have one, find a beautiful hideaway in nature
where you can be at peace. Visit it often.

There is a story of a Zen monk who was chased by
a hungry tiger. He sought refuge by climbing down a cliff
and hanging on a branch above a ledge occupied by yet
another tiger. He was trapped. If he climbed back up, the first tiger
would devour him. If he let go and dropped to the ledge underneath,
he would be lunch for the tiger below.
Within arm's reach, a single ripe strawberry
hung from another branch. He picked it, admired its color,
put it in his mouth, and savored it slowly, exclaiming,
"How tasty it is!"

When you feel overwhelmed,
remember this story. Immerse yourself in the moment.
Taste it. Smell it. Hear it. Feel it. See it. Experience it.

THE GIFT OF TIME

. . . .

"That which is timeless is found now."

—*Buddha*

There is no such thing as a little moment.
It is those moments that appear least significant that
can be the most extraordinary.
The next time you see a flower,
admire its beauty, color, and form.
Breathe its fragrance deeply.
Wonder at its ability to live, grow,
and open to your love.

Sand flows through the hourglass

one grain at a time.

and life is meant to be lived

one moment at a time.